The Top 10 Everyday Tools

For

Daily Problem-Solving

Discover the Key Basics of Life

The Simplicity
of
Systems Thinking

Stephen G. Haines

The Top 10 EVERYDAY Tools

For

Daily Problem-Solving

The Systems Thinking Approach™

CENTRE
FOR
STRATEGIC
MANAGEMENT®

Dear Systems Thinking Reader:

Welcome to Systems Thinking—"A New Orientation to Work and Life."

As a way to begin your progression to the "Systems Age," this Handbook is the first in our series outlining the concepts of Systems Thinking. You will find the tools you need to shift to a new, unique, and better way to think, act, and achieve results.

We recommend a one-day *Executive Briefing Session* with the Centre for Strategic Management® to help your training in Systems Thinking. During this one-day with your team, we help you work through all 10 tools and their corresponding worksheets.

- Use these tools every day at work on any change project you are implementing.

- Use these same tools every day at home or at play in your life.

Happy thinking... and acting... and better results!

[signature: Stephen S. Haines]

Stephen Haines, Founder and CEO
Centre for Strategic Management®
San Diego, California • www.csmintl.com
(619) 275-6528 • stephen@csmintl.com

P.S. To understand Systems Thinking fully, please ask us about:

- Strategic Thinking Handbook #2: "The Top 10 Tools for Everyday Use at Work and Play"

- "The Manager's Pocket Guide to Systems Thinking"

- The Comprehensive Reference Library, Volume VIII on *"Systems Thinking (also on CD-ROM and fully reproducible"*

- Plus our many other management books on the Systems Thinking Approach™ to Strategic Management (Planning - People - Leadership - Change).

Check them out on our website: www.SystemsThinkingPress.com

TABLE OF CONTENTS

Daily Problem-Solving

Dear Reader,

We'd like you to look at the earth as the astronauts do – 260 miles above the surface – with a holistic view of Earth as a living planet, floating out in space, with all its major natural characteristics visible. Actually, you don't even need to be an astronaut—you can get this same view flying in a helicopter high above ground level.

So, we'd like you to visualize getting into a helicopter and climbing up to 5000 feet. This perspective will help you enormously in understanding the tools in this book by giving you a better and higher vantage point on life and work, virtually improving your practical and strategic IQ by over 50 points.

We will use this helicopter analogy throughout to remind you of how to read and understand Systems Thinking as... *"A New Orientation to Life."*

> "Many attend, but few understand."
> — *Martin Luther King, Jr.*

The words "systems thinking" are used a lot these days. They mean different things to different people. Often, they are used simply to mean there is a checklist of things that somehow relate to each other. That is *not* Systems Thinking but a different way of thinking, called "analytic thinking," or just "thinking" to many of you.

If you read this book and use these tools from the *helicopter point of view*, you can be one of a growing number of professionals who *really* understand the deeper meaning of Systems Thinking and all its elegant simplicity.

Here's to Strategic Thinking!

Stephen G. Haines

Our Level of Thinking

"Problems that are created by our current level of thinking can't be solved by that same level of thinking."

— *Albert Einstein*

"So...if we generally use analytical thinking, we now need real 'Systems Thinking' to resolve our issues."

— *Stephen Haines*

Get a Higher and Broader Perspective
for
Better Problem Solving

Take a Helicopter View of Life!

Network of Mutuality

"We are tied together in the single
garment of destiny, caught in an inescapable
network of mutuality."
                                — *Martin Luther King, Jr.*

The Top 10 **EVERYDAY** Tools
For
Daily Problem-Solving

SECTION I:

Overview
of
Systems Thinking

Discover the Key Basics of Life

ANALYTIC THINKING

"From an early age, we're taught
to break apart problems in order to make
complex tasks and subjects easier to deal with.
But this creates a bigger problem...
we lose the ability to see the consequences
of our actions, and we lose a sense of
connection to a larger whole."

— Peter Senge, The Fifth Discipline

A Basic Reorientation
of Our Thinking is Needed

"In one way or another, we are forced to deal
with complexities, with 'wholes' or 'systems'
in all fields of knowledge.
This implies a basic reorientation in
scientific thinking."

— Ludwig Van Bertalanffy

ANALYTIC vs. SYSTEMS THINKING

Although the dominant view in our lives is "Analytic Thinking," the *Natural Order of the World and Life on Earth* is a SYSTEMS one. Analytic approaches to systems problems are *bankrupt* in our society and organizations!

The good news is that a more effective approach, "Systems Thinking," is rapidly emerging. Witness the increased use of systems-oriented words such as:

■ United	■ Linkages
■ Fit	■ Stakeholders
■ Integration	■ Holistic
■ Collaboration	■ Seamless
■ Cooperation	
■ Teamwork	■ Boundaryless
■ Partnerships	■ System
■ Alliances	■ Synergistic

Machine-Age Fundamental Assumptions Are Wrong

Systems Thinking is about looking at life in a new way—synergistically, so that 2+2 = 5.

Analytic thinking, when paired with reductionism, does make us 'micro-smart' – good at thinking through component parts and elements – but it also makes us 'macro-dumb,' so we're not good at looking at the whole situation from the helicopter or (even better) the astronaut's point of view.

PRINCIPLES OF LIVING SYSTEMS

1. **System Clarity First** — The system or entity to be problem-solved must be clearly identified.

2. **The Whole is Primary** — The whole is primary and the parts are secondary. Focusing on maximizing the parts leads to suboptimizing the whole.

3. **Understand Systems Holistically in Their Environment** — Systems, and organizations as systems, can only be understood holistically. Try to understand the system and its environment first. Organizations are open systems and, as such, are viable only in mutual interaction with, and adaptation to, the changing environment.

4. **Each System Functions Uniquely** — Every system has properties or functions that none of its parts can do.

5. **System Purposes First** — The place to start is with the whole and its purposes within its environment. The parts and their relationships evolve from this.

6. **The Role of Parts: To Support the Whole** — Parts play their role in light of the purpose for which the whole exists. Focus on the desired outcomes; not just the problems of the parts.

7. **All Parts Are Interdependent** — Parts, elements, and subsystems are interdependent...a web of relationships. Therefore, yesterday's great solutions may lead to today's issues. No system can be subdivided into independent parts. A system as a whole cannot function effectively when it loses a part.

8. **Small Changes Produce Big Results** — Change in any element of a system affects the whole as well as the other subsystems. The smallest changes can produce big results if the leverage points are clear.

9. **Maximizing Parts Suboptimizes the Whole** — Exclusive focus on one element or subsystem without simultaneous attention to other subsystems leads to suboptimal results and new disturbances. The solution or simple cure can often be worse than the real disease.

10. **Causes and Effects Are Not Closely Related** — Delay-time and delayed reactions cause inaccurate diagnoses and solutions. Cause and effect are not as closely related in time and space as most of us think.

11. Faster is Ultimately Slower — Systems have a natural pace to them. Sometimes trying to go faster is ultimately slower.

12. Feedback — The more feedback systems receive, the more "open" they are and the more likely they are to sustain their existence longer and more effectively.

13. Multiple Goals — All systems have multiple goals. Building consensus on those goals first is the key to achieving them. It is also the key to successful teamwork.

14. Flexibility — People can achieve their goals and outcomes in many different ways—thus the Centre for Strategic Management's "strategic consistency – operational flexibility" concept of the 21st Century.

15. Hierarchy is Natural — Despite some recent political correctness against hierarchies, all systems have a natural hierarchy. Find it, minimize it, and make it work for you.

16. Entropy and the Tendency to Run Down — All systems have a tendency towards maximum entropy, disorder and death. Importing resources from the environment is the key to long-term viability; closed systems move toward this disorganization faster than open systems.

Summary

So: A system cannot be understood by analysis, but by synthesis; looking at it as a whole within its environment.

Thus: In organizations we don't deal with problems—we deal with "messes of problems."

Messes of Problems

"Effective managers do not solve problems.
They dissolve messes."

— *Dr. Russell L. Ackoff, Chairman, Interact*

Stop Using "Analytic Approaches to Systems Problems"

Systems vs. Analytic Thinking

In Systems Thinking — the whole is primary and the parts are secondary.

In Analytic Thinking — the parts are primary and the whole is secondary.

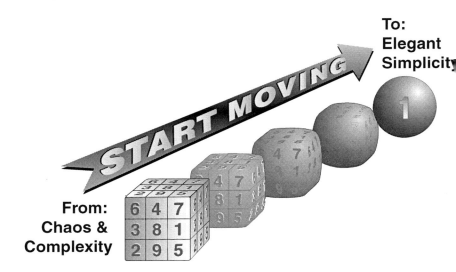

To: Elegant Simplicity

START MOVING

From: Chaos & Complexity

6	4	7
3	8	1
2	9	5

SECTION II:

The Key Basics

of

Daily Problem-Solving

O━━┳

Discover the Key Basics of Life

Better Problem-Solving

"If life on earth is governed
by the natural laws of living systems,
then a successful participant should learn
the rules."

— *Stephen Haines*

Thus:

The Systems Thinking
Approach™ is an absolute
necessity to succeed in
today's complex world.

— *Stephen Haines*

<u>TOOL #1:</u>

Clarify the System To Be Problem-Solved

"What entity, system or 'collision' of systems are we dealing with?"

TOOL #1: Clarify the System

Identify which overall system or systems you are trying to problem solve (which organization, alliance, partnership, business process etc.). Also be clear on its boundaries and limitations. Where does begin and end?

While this question may seem so obvious that it doesn't even nee to be asked, people's thought processes can be so unclear that thi question must be asked as a *precondition* to any intelligent and e fective action. First ask: *"What entity, system, or 'collision' of sy tems are we dealing with?"*

> ### Principle
> ## System Clarity First
> *The system or entity to be problem-solved*
> *must be clearly identified first!*

Challenge the obvious—always look for, and identify, which of the Seven Levels of Living Systems you're dealing with. Be clear or the entity you are working to problem-solve. Is it an individual, de partment, team, family, project team, business unit, community organization, company, state, nation or international entity? Wha are its boundaries? Is it relatively open or closed in its environ mental interactions?

Remember, individuals and organizations need to focus on the fol lowing levels or activities:

Which System(s) or Level(s) to Focus Upon?	
#3	Self
#3A	One-to-One
#4	Work Teams
#4A	Between Departments
#5	Total Organizations
#5A	Organization-Environment or Society

#7
Earth

#6
Society

#5
Total
Organizations

#4
Work
Teams

#3
Self

#2
Organ

#1
Cell

EXAMPLES

Tool #1: Clarify The System

Workplace example:

The biggest problem-solving failure is often the "Team-to-Team" Level #4 – horizontally across departments.

One team decided to simplify a time-consuming report they submitted weekly to three other departments. They restructured their workflow and reduced the time it took to collect the data and collate the report by 1/3. After the fact, we helped them get up in that helicopter and look at their report one system removed from their intra-team perspective. When we surveyed the three departments to whom they submitted this data, we discovered the report and it's format were relics of past practices. Two of the departments no longer needed the data, and the third would have preferred to have the raw data to work with!

▶ At life and play example:

Auto mechanics, plumbers,and electricians all use their knowledge of the larger system to limit the number of options they need to

investigate to identify the problem causing the symptoms reported
Ever wonder why "Click and Clack" (Tom and Ray Magliozzi of the
NPR Radio Program "Car Talk") always manage to solve the
mysterious mechanical and electrical problems posed by their
callers? They use the process of elimination to determine exactly
where the malfunction has to occur in the system to cause the
symptoms!

General Purposes at Each Level

Level #3: Individuals ("Self-Mastery")

- Improve personal competency and effectiveness.
- Explore trust issues within us.

Level #3A: One-to-One Relationships (Interpersonal Skills)

- Improve the interpersonal and working relationships and
  effectiveness of each individual.
- Address trust issues between us.

Level #4: Work Teams and Groups (Team Effectiveness)

- Improve the effectiveness of the work team as well as its individual members.
- Investigate empowerment and interpersonal roles and issues.

Level #4A: Intergroups (Conflict and Horizontal Cooperation)

- Improve the working relationships and business processes
  across teams or departments horizontally to serve the
  customer better.
- Address horizontal collaboration and integration issues.

Level #5: Total Organization (Fit)

- Improve the organization's systems, structures, and processes
  to better achieve its business results and potential.
- Develop the organization's capacity to provide an adaptive system of change and response to a changing environment while
  pursuing its vision and strategic plan.
- Address issues of alignment.

Level #5A: Organization-Environment (Marketplace Survival)

■ Improve the organization's sense of direction, response to its customers and proactive management of the environment and stakeholders by reinventing strategic planning for the 21st Century.

■ Adapt to environmental issues.

USES

▶ Problem-solving will be very different at each of the different levels. Personal change solutions are different from team or family changes, which are different from organizational change.

▶ Troubleshoot all solutions to see what change you predict they will bring—in your personal or your organizational life. Can you predict that the answers you have chosen will achieve the desired changes? How do they relate to the environment?

Organizational change to create high performance organizations requires paying attention to all the levels of systems within the organization and all the interactions of systems colliding with other systems. There are different solutions at each of these levels, and each is important to success.

▶ Engineer success up front by clarifying which levels and purposes you are trying to problem-solve, as well as other levels you will need to change to achieve your desired outcomes.

TOOL #1 SUMMARY

First, clarify the system or entity
you are trying to problem-solve.

Worksheet #1

I. At Work

1. What issue am I problem-solving at work?

   _____

2. Which level of systems is it?

   _____

3. What are the implications of problem-solving at this level?

   a)_____

   b)_____

   c)_____

   d)_____

II. At Life & Play

1. What am I problem-solving or tolerating in my life?

   _____

2. Which level of systems is it?

   _____

3. What are the implications of problem-solving at this level?

   a)_____

   b)_____

   c)_____

   d)_____

TOOL #2:

Focus on
Systems Solutions vs.
Problem-Solving

Ask: "What solutions achieve our objectives or outcomes?"

NOT:
"What solves our problem?"

TOOL #2: Focus on Systems Solutions

Our A-B-C Systems Model – Simplicity

It is much more effective to use a systems-oriented, "solution-seeking" model that focuses on objectives or outcomes verses the traditional problem-solving model. You will also find the "solution-seeking" model useful when trouble-shooting for potential side-effects of any given solution.

Living Systems are naturally input-processes-output systems. We use our A-B-C Systems Model to illustrate how these systems operate. The question is: Does this model represent your orientation to life? (It should

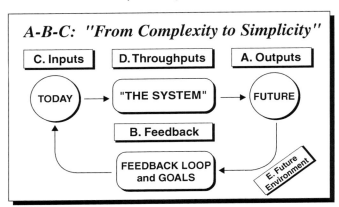

Principle

System Purposes First

The place to start is with the whole and its purposes within its environment. The parts and their relationships evolve from this.

Use of Our A-B-C Systems Model

Analyze and solve problems within the context of your desired outcomes using our A-B-C Systems Model:

A **Start by asking:** Where do you ideally want to be (desired outcomes)?
   Then, use Backwards Thinking:

B How will you know you've gotten there (measurable goals)?

C Where are you now (today's issues and problems)?

D How do you get from where you are to where you want to be?

E **And, ongoing:** What may change in your environment in the future?

24

"SYSTEMS SOLUTIONS ARE CIRCULAR..."

... they achieve desired future outcomes
... they fit within their environment
... they don't just solve today's problems

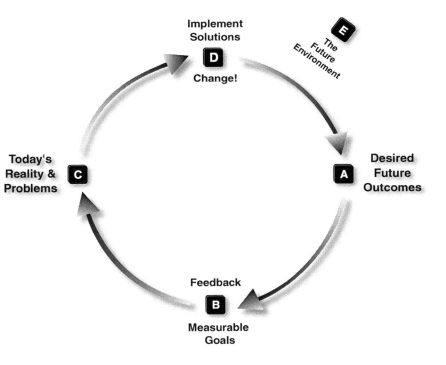

Solution-Seeking Sequence: 7 Steps

[C] 1. **Identify problem or issue today**— root causes, not simpl
cause and effect.

Now Use Systems (and Backwards) Thinking:

[A] 2. **Set ideal desired objectives** or goals that also solve the roo
causes (usually a weakness in analytic thinking).
[E] ■ Within your scanning of the relevant environment.
[B] ■ With quantifiable outcome measures of success.

[C] 3. **Brainstorm alternative strategies** or actions to achieve these
ideal outcomes or desired solutions (usually a weakness i
analytic thinking).
■ There's always a third alternative. Find it.
■ Be sure to collect data and facts about the issues.

4. **Develop first draft of strategies** and integrated action plans

Double back:

[D] 5. **Troubleshoot the integrated action plans** (usually a weak
ness in analytic thinking).
■ Examine your biases and assumptions.
[E] ■ **Check the environment** related to the decision, both
internally and externally.
■ Include a "Parallel Process" with key stakeholders to
increase buy-in and ownership, and generate more ideas
for correct systems solutions.
■ Remember about the "relationships" of all parts to each
other and the overall objectives.

[D] 6. **Implement action plans** with speed and flexibility.
■ Include roll-out and communications.

[D] 7. **Continually provide feedback** about how close you are t
meeting your goals. Give frequent status updates. Timing an
goals may change, given the complex and changing environ
ments that you are dealing with.

EXAMPLES

Tool #2: Focus on Systems Solutions

Workplace example:

Work teams are encouraged to consider their "mission" to ensure that they understand both "who" their customer is and "what" their deliverable is. **A hospital, for example, might have a mission to provide patients with the "best possible healthcare experience."** Assuming the health care is of the highest quality, what will leave the patient feeling they've had the best experience? Research shows that THE most discriminating factor for patient satisfaction, medical services being equal, is a choice of food at mealtime. It isn't even the quality of the food patients respond to, but fact they are given a choice.

At life and play example:

Is your goal to have a healthy life? Well, modern medicine has taught us a great deal about heart disease, cholesterol, diabetes, high blood pressure, colon cancer, toxin build-up, complexion care and diet. Things get complicated when we look at our bodies as a series of sub-systems – circulatory, respiratory, elimination... But there IS a point of commonality – the primary cleansing system: the liver! If we eat a diet known to be healthy for our liver, the rest of our bodily functions protect the other subsystems. Be good to your liver, and you're being good to yourself and your goal of a healthy life!

USES

► Learn the "Solution-Seeking" Model.

► Use it instead of a traditional problem-solving model.

► Focus especially on Steps 2, 3, and 5—the weak areas in most problem-solving.

O━ㅠ

TOOL #2 SUMMARY

Focus first on your objectives and outcomes.

Be solutions-oriented vs. just problem-solving today's issue.

Be sure to trouble-shoot solutions before you implement them.

Worksheet #2

At Work or Play

1. What problem do you have at work or play?
    _____

2. What are your desired outcomes?
    _____

3. Brainstorm some alternative actions to achieve these outcomes:
    _____
    _____
    _____
    _____
    _____

4. Pick two or three actions that you think will help you achieve your outcomes:
    _____
    _____
    _____

5. Trouble-shoot these actions yourself or with a trusted friend:
    _____
    _____
    _____

6. How will you implement these actions? By when?
    _____
    _____
    _____

7. How can you get feedback during implementation to ensure success?
    _____

TOOL #3:

Simplicity in Project Management

"How can we scope out our project in advance using the simple A-B-C Systems Model?"

TOOL #3: Simplicity In Project Management

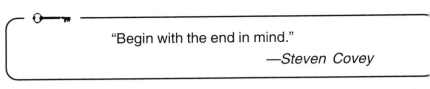

> "Begin with the end in mind."
>
> —*Steven Covey*

Parts, elements, and subsystems are interdependent...a web of relationships. Therefore, yesterday's great solutions may lead to today' issues. No system can be subdivided into independent parts. I addition, a system as a whole cannot function effectively when loses a part.

Principle

All Parts Are Interdependent

Parts, elements, subsystems are interdependent...
a web of relationships. Therefore, yesterday's great solutions
may lead to today's issues. No system can be subdivided
into independent parts. A system as a whole cannot function
effectively when it loses a parts.

Because all parts are interrelated, it is important to look at them a when managing a project. No matter what kind of a project you ar managing, keep in mind that our A-B-C Model represents a "Nev Orientation to Life."

EXAMPLES

Tool #3: Simplicity in Project Management

▶ **Workplace example:**

Using the A-B-C Model to thoroughly scope out a project before begins helps us to clarify the outcome of the project, the strategie we'll use to reach the outcomes, and the measurements that wi define project success. The "backwards thinking" approach provide all the tools we need to realign a project when changes occur i the intended outcome (customer changes order), the environmer (technology or political issues), or in the resources available fc the project (budget cuts, schedule adjustments, testing delays).

At life and play example:

We've all tackled a simple home project like cleaning out the garage only to have it mushroom out of control when we unearthed a series of time consuming distractions: that old lawn mower that we might spent ½ hour trying to start, a bicycle with one bent rim we ran to the sporting goods store to replace, and a pile of old clothes we started sorting through. Suddenly the sun has gone down, half the contents of the garage are still in the driveway, and you've made little progress "cleaning out the garage!" Using Systems Thinking for home projects helps us identify possible distractions up front, and have a plan to stay on track and finish the job. So, what was your original desired outcome?

JSES

For problem-solving and project management, set out the following A-B-C model of Worksheet #3 on the next three pages (copy these three originals to use over and over again).

Use them as a guide to address all five phases and their associated questions.

Share them and gain consensus with:
■ All key project members.
■ All project sponsors and stakeholders.

Then begin!

The Five Phases of our A-B-C Systems Model:

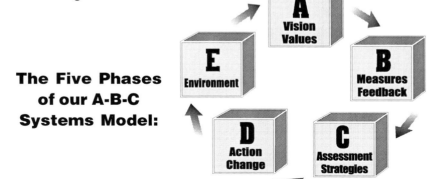

Daily Problem-Solving

Worksheet #3

A Desired Outcomes of Project (Work or Life?)

1. _____

2. _____

3. _____

B Key Success Measures or "Goals:"

1. _____

2. _____

3. _____

C List your Project's **Current State Assessment** (or SWOT): List your top three for each category: **S**trengths, **W**eaknesses, **O**pportunities, **T**hreats)

INTERNAL

S (Strengths) the project has:	**W** (Weaknesses) the project has:
1. _____	1. _____
2. _____	2. _____
3. _____	3. _____

EXTERNAL

O (Opportunities) of the project:	**T** (Threats) to the project:
1. _____	1. _____
2. _____	2. _____
3. _____	3. _____

TOOL #3: Simplicity in Project Management

Worksheet #3

D Project Strategies and Actions:

Strategies	Top 3 Actions
1.	1. 2. 3.
2.	1. 2. 3.
3.	1. 2. 3.
4.	1. 2. 3.
5.	1. 2. 3.
6.	1. 2. 3.

| Worksheet #3 | page 3/3 |

D Project Timeline For Implementation

Beginning Date   Milestone   Ending Date

Details:
_____
_____
_____
_____
_____

E Within What Changing Environments?
_____
_____
_____
_____
_____
_____

TOOL #3 SUMMARY

- Use Backwards Thinking and the A-B-C Model to scope out all projects in advance.

- To achieve your objectives, solution-seeking is much more effective than problem-solving.

TOOL #4:

Use the Right Matrix

*"What relationships
(of all the parts)
does your matrix
reveal?"*

TOOL #4: Use the Right Matrix

Systems Thinking is all about relationships, components and thei impact on the whole. **A matrix reveals the relationships of all the parts to each other.** It ensures that a comprehensive analysis an action plan are developed—a classic Systems Thinking format. Ma trices are great to show the relationships between systems and/o parts of systems.

A matrix is key to achieving better results from projects, change efforts, and any other complex issues. Organizations are comple systems–a matrix is vital to unlocking the mysteries of these com plexities.

Principle

Maximizing Parts Suboptimizes the Whole

Exclusive focus on one element or subsystem
without simultaneous attention to other subsystems
leads to suboptimal results and new disturbances.
The solution or simple cure can often
be worse than the real disease.

Principle

The Role of Parts: To Support the Whole

Parts play their role in light of
the purpose for which the whole exists.
Focus on the desired outcomes; not just the
problems of the parts.

"Action planning" and solution-seeking becomes easier once yo establish the proper matrix and analyze the relationships.

"A Lattice Fence (Matrix)
Is Very Strong"

USES

▶ Use a **Strategic Communications Matrix** for communicatin strategically about your changes to all stakeholders.

How Who	Face-to-Face	Large Group Meeting	Video	Voice Mail	E-mail	Written Letter	Feed-back
Middle Mngmt.							
1st Line Supvsr.							
All Depts.							
All Employees							
List Key Stake-holders							

▶ **Organizational Life Cycle Matrix:**
1. Use this cycle to give an accurate view of your organization current stage of development. Constant feedback and enviroi ment scanning fights off decline and enhances renewal oppo tunities.

2. What implications does your current position have on futui strategies? (Each stage requires a different strategy. See tr Centre's book, *Strategy School* for more details.)

Competitive ↓ Position	Company Maturity				
	1. Startup	2. Growth	3. Mature	4. Decline	5. Renewal
A. Dominant					
B. Leading					
C. Important					
D. Tenable					
E. Weak					

TOOL #4: Use the Right Matrix

Change Management Plan: Fill out columns two and three using High, Medium or Low for your answers. Note any ideas or comments in the last column.

Explicit Tasks	Emphasis in last two years	Need for Improvement	Comments
1. Strategy/ Accountability			
2. Quality/Service			
3. Leadership & Strategic Communications			
4. Organizational Capabilities			
5. Resources: Critical Mass for Change			
6. HR Processes			
7. Teams			
8. Overall: Culture of Change			
9. Feedback: Assess/ Sustain Change			
10. Mega Track: Change Process			

Customer Value Current Assessment: Use this format to assess what your customers currently value and how you are currently meeting these desires, by customer segments.

Assessment of What Customer Values / Customer Segments	Score 1 (Low) to 10 (High)				
	#1 Individual Choice and Control	#2 Caring Service and Relationships	#3 Quality Products and Services	#4 Delivery, Speed, and Convenience	#5 Low Total Cost
1.					
2.					
3.					
4.					

EXAMPLE

TOOL #4: Use the Right Matrix

▶ At life and play example:

A terrific application of a matrix is the "chore list." On one side o the matrix you have each family member. On the other side yo list the daily chores. An "X" in the box indicates who is assigne what chore! Or you can use the third dimension of the matrix t assign a different chore to a different individual each week. Us the same format for holiday gift giving, who gets to choose T programs or who helps whom with homework!

	Garbage Out	Feed Dog	Wash Dishes	Do Laundry
Mom	Week 1	Week 2	Week 3	Week 4
Dad	Week 2	Week 3	Week 4	Week 1
Tommy	Week 3	Week 4	Week 1	Week 2
Sally	Week 4	Week 1	Week 2	Week 3

USES

▶ The use of a matrix is vital in virtually all issues, projects anc problems. How?

1. Set up a matrix comprised of the components or systems you want to analyze regarding a specific issue.

2. On the matrix, list the relationship between each componen shown in the left-hand column that interacts with the com ponents shown along the top row (i.e., fill-in each box of the matrix). What conclusions can you draw from this exercise?

3. Develop action plans as a result of what you see.

TOOL #4 SUMMARY

Consider using a matrix in analyzing the relationships of all parts of a problem, project or issue. A matrix reveals the root causes, core issues and direction of the correct solutions.

TOOL #5:

Look in the Mirror
(Self Feedback)

*"What am I doing
(or not doing) that is
helping to cause the
problem?"*

"To be the best, you have to be totally honest
with yourself...and others."

—*Thurman Thomas,*
Professional Football Hall of Fame

TOOL #5: Look in the Mirror

Self-Mastery

Self-Feedback

Focus on your own role in any problem. We are a
interdependent and independent at the same time. So first, workin
independently, look inward at yourself to determine the problem an
some solutions—don't look for others to blame.

Principle

Feedback

The more feedback systems receive,
the more "open" they are and the more likely they
are to sustain their existence longer and more effectively.

See yourself as the object that is the problem, and "problem-solve
yourself. The world would be a far better place if each of us cou
only change one individual each—ourselves!

The individual must change in order for the organization to change
The first individuals to change must be people in charge at ever
level. Leaders must "walk the talk"—*be* the right role model.

EXAMPLE

The Wise Person and the Fool:

Question: What's the difference between the wise person an
the fool?

Answer: They both make mistakes, but the wise person con
tinually learns from his/her own mistakes and experiences, a
well as from those of others.

"Let him who would move the world
first move himself."

—*Socrates*

> "He who knows others is learned;
> he who knows himself is wise."
> —*Lao Tzu*

Seeking Feedback

Feedback is vitally important. Do you seek it individually and collectively to make sure you are focusing on the right outcomes, even when the feedback might be painful? Constant feedback is what creates the competitive advantage of the Learning Organization . . . and the Learning Individual.

The key is encouraging feedback about your performance—from others as well as from yourself. Accept feedback gracefully:

1. Tolerate pain
2. Search for the truth
3. Have humility
4. Accept feedback gracefully

EXAMPLES

Tool #5: Look in the Mirror

▶ **Workplace example:**

Enlisting a co-worker's (or even your manager's) help in improving your performance is as easy as asking for it! It takes courage to ask, but the rewards will be enormous. Here are some ways you might ask for feedback:

- "How could I have handled that better?"
- "That didn't go well. Can you offer me any advice?"
- "Can we set up a time to go over what just happened? I think need to learn some new ways of handling situations like that."
- "I feel badly about the way I reacted and the fact that it upset you. It would really help me if you'd promise to call me on it if i happens again."
- "I can see you're upset about what I said, and I'm sorry. Are you willing to tell me how it made you feel?"
- "What just happened may have been insensitive on my part What did it feel like to you?"
- "If I hurt your feelings it was unintentional. Help me understand how I hurt you."

▶ **At life and play example:**

Relationships need the same care at work and at home. Try these same questions with your spouse, your children, your friends and other members of the community with whom you interact!

Intellectual honesty is the key!

Balancing "advocacy and inquiry" is crucial to individual learning.

Inquiry is in the spirit of non-judgmental feedback, curiosity, an new learning. Dialogue, discovery, and the search for truth are th outcomes for self-mastery.

Advocacy, instead, is trying to influence others toward your poi of view and judgment.

Many people spend much of their time defending their point of view. They look to blame others and don't listen to, or care about, the views of family members, friends, or colleagues.

On the other hand, if you are intellectually honest with yourself and focus on your desired outcomes (which usually include growth and learning), you will find that the path of "inquiry" and curiosity is a better way to live your life. Being open to discovery will help you grow and learn so much more.

USES

Commit yourself to "intellectual honesty," even if you can't always tell others. Be honest with yourself in your own mind.

Know your own strengths and weaknesses. Look at yourself first to define the problems and root causes.

The key in any problem-solving is to suspend judgment at first and to collect more data. Advocate only after you've learned all you can from others.

O━━▅

TOOL #5 SUMMARY

Two major things to learn about change:

1. *The only thing we can change is our own behavior.* We cannot change anyone else's. The word "behavior" in layman's language, means simply what we *do*.
2. *We must assume responsibility for our own destiny.* We cannot blame anyone else for our misfortunes.

Don't ask the wrong question:

The old question was: *"What are your problems?"*

The new question is: ***"What am I doing (or not doing) that's helping to cause the problem?"***

Worksheet #5

I. At Work

1. Identify a problem you are having with someone at work:

   _____

2. Look in the mirror first: what part did you play in contributing to the problem?

   _____
   _____
   _____
   _____
   _____
   _____

II. At Play & Life

1. Identify a problem you are having with someone in your life:

   _____

2. Look in the mirror first: what part did you play in contributing to the problem?

   _____
   _____
   _____
   _____
   _____
   _____

TOOL #6:

"People Support What They Help Create"

"Who are the key 'stakeholders' to involve in solving this problem?"

One-To-One Relationships

The Power in Participation

"People support what they help create"—an extremely importan statement for powerful problem-solving and "solution-seeking." Peopl want to be involved and give input into decisions that affect them before the final decision is made.

As part of your process, involve all key employees affected b potential problem-solving solutions.

⌐ Principle ─────────────────────────

Faster Is Ultimately Slower

Systems have a natural pace to them.
Sometimes trying to go faster is ultimately slower.

A decision-making goal should always be to:

■ Arrive at the best possible decision.

■ Gain as much support as you can for the decision from all those who are involved or affected by the decision.

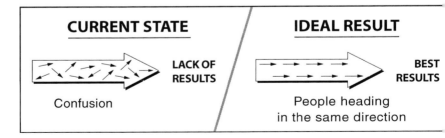

CURRENT STATE	IDEAL RESULT
LACK OF RESULTS	BEST RESULTS
Confusion	People heading in the same direction

Involving others may take more time when problem-solving However, the solution will ultimately be achieved faster due to les resistance.

"Skeptics Are My Best Friends"--

Why?

What we need are participative problem-solvers—those wh•
gather input on issues from the people who will be affected, befor•
the decisions have been made. This requires asking questions an•
listening openly to the answers, whether you like them or not. The•
you must be willing to adopt new ideas.

"What must be abandoned by organizations is
a whole ideology, a whole way of thinking about power.
Power no longer belongs in boxes, in titles, in ranks.
What counts for power is what you do yourself
with your own skills."

— *Jim Champy, Reengineering Management*

EXAMPLES

Tool #6: People Support What They Help Create

▶ **Workplace example:**

Everyone has experienced the frustration of learning about
decision that greatly impacted you, but you were never aske•
about your opinion. Often, we can clearly see a problem that th•
decision makers didn't even consider. Don't make that mistak•
yourself. If you are designing, deciding, implementing o•
prioritizing, ask yourself three critical questions: 1) Who will b•
affected? 2) Who believes they will be affected? 3) What coul•
possibly go wrong, and who might that impact? Then find a wa•
to include ALL of those people in the discussion process.

▶ **At work and play example:**

Who can be more resistant to change than children? Is your chi•
changing schools? Are you moving – to a new home or even •
new city? How can you involve your children in making ke•
decisions about the new school, new house or activities they•
enjoy in the new location? How can you involve them in th•
planning, decision-making, discussions about the change?

USES

Building a Critical Mass for Change

1. It can take a long time to build a critical mass of support for large scale change. The following are some ways to help you do this:

   - Modify Project Plan drafts — listen, review (share and gain feedback) from those affected.

   - Continue to hold meetings with key stakeholders throughout planning and implementation.

   - Develop trust in your project team by being open—involve "skeptics" and listen to them every day. *Skeptics are our best friends!* They know why the project might fail.

2. Ensure that annual plans for all departments, divisions, and sections include your project as one of the corporate priorities for the year.

3. Create "updates" after each project team meeting and ask for feedback from skeptics and other key stakeholders.

4. Implement quick changes or actions right away so people know you are serious. *Generate Momentum!*

5. Answer WIIFM *("What's In It For Me")* for each person – looking at issues from their point of view. Understand it, too!

TOOL #6 SUMMARY

"People Support What They Help Create"

Remember: **"Skeptics are our best friends."** If you encounter skeptics, involve them. Be sure to ask them why they are skeptical. Get them to identify the road blocks. Don't try to force them to agree with you. Consider solutions that will answer and solve their doubts and you will be more successful.

Worksheet #6

At Work or Play

1. Identify an issue or problem you need to solve:

    _____

    _____

2. Identify the key stakeholders and skeptics:

    _____   _____

    _____   _____

    _____   _____

    _____   _____

3. List three ways to involve them in problem-solving:

    a) _____

    _____

    _____

    _____

    b) _____

    _____

    _____

    _____

    c) _____

    _____

    _____

    _____

TOOL #7:

Process All Meetings

*"How did your
meeting go?"*

*"Learn from them –
Continuous Improvement"*

TOOL #7: Process All Meetings

Team Mini-Feedback

At the end of every meeting, training, problem-solving, or grou
session held in an organization, there should be a short, 3-minut
feedback session on how the meeting went and how to improve it

---
Principle

Small Changes Produce Big Results

*Change in any element of a system affects the whole,
as well as other subsystems. The smallest changes can
produce big results if the leverage points are clear.*

In order to maximize the efficiency of meetings, process how well
went and whether you achieved your goals at the end of every mee
ing. Learn from your past experiences—continuous improvement
key! Remember, change in any element of a system affects the whol
so even the smallest changes can produce big results.

EXAMPLES

Tool #7: Process All Meetings

▶ **Workplace example:**

The best salespeople do a thorough, personal "debriefing" aft
every sales meeting, even with a long-term client. What did I ju
learn about my client? What products did they express intere
in? What did I say that made them lose interest, even if only briefl
What should I be prepared to show him/her, or tell him/her ne
time we meet? You can apply this technique to any meetin
whether you lead it or not. If you lead the meeting, engage
participants in the debriefing. Be sure to summarize not only wh
you've learned, but how you will use what you've learned to impro
the next meeting!

At life and play example:

People are constantly growing and changing. Making sure that we have an up-to-date perception of the people we live and play with takes effort on our part. It's so easy, especially with family members, to develop a conviction that we know these people very well. Not leaving room for them to grow can be a major source of conflict. Pay attention to the words they use, the thoughts they express, the questions they ask. Look for clues into the ways they are changing. Ask them about it in ways that are supportive of their continued growth. Find the right time and place.

USES

Meeting Processing Guide

1. Write the following three questions, *in the order shown be low,* on a flip chart and have meeting participants answe them in rapid-fire fashion.

2. "Considering the past __60__ minutes (or __3__ hours) we've just spent meeting, let's make the next meeting work eve better. Answer the following questions..."

Meeting Processing Guide – Continuous Improvement

"In order for our next meeting to be even more effective, I recommend we:"

1. Continue to do (the following):

2. Do more of (or begin doing):

3. Do less of (or stop doing):

Using the Meeting Processing Guide takes only a few minutes, an you receive useful feedback to improve immediately.

JSES

At the end of every meeting, conference, training day or project effort, ask your group the three "Meeting Processing Guide" questions (in order).

The fourth and final question to ask after a meeting is:

4. "If you were talking to a good friend after the meeting, what would you say about the meeting?"

If you have more time, you can also ask the following additional questions:

5. "How did you feel about this meeting?"

6. "On a scale of 1-10 (with 1 being the low and 10 being high), how satisfied were you with the meeting?"

7. "How are we doing vs. our "norms" or "ground rules" for holding effective meetings?"

8. "What one or two things could we incorporate that would move your score one to two points higher?"

○──ᴍ

TOOL #7 SUMMARY

Be Adaptable and Flexible

"It is not the strongest of the species that survive.
Nor is it the most intelligent,
but the one most responsive to change."

—*Charles Darwin*

Use the "Rule of Three"

Ask three questions at the end of every meeting.

—*Stephen Haines*

Worksheet #7

I. At Work

Think of the last meeting you attended. List your responses to these three key questions:

1. What should we continue to do?

_____

_____

2. What should we do more of (or begin doing)?

_____

_____

3. What should we do less of (or stop doing)?

_____

_____

II. At Play & Life

Think of a meeting or dinner or family gathering you have attended in your life recently. List your responses to these three key questions:

1. What should we continue to do?

_____

_____

2. What should we do more of (or begin doing)?

_____

_____

3. What should we do less of (or stop doing)?

_____

_____

TOOL #8:

Debrief All Projects/Conflicts

"How can we learn from this project (or conflict)?"

TOOL #8: Debrief All Projects/Conflicts

Debriefing

Feedback vs. Desired Outcomes. In most organizations, the pressur of time gets in the way of learning from our experiences. We finish th task at hand and rush on to the next, oblivious to true, in-depth learnin. In its place, each person takes his or her own perception to the ne task, without checking these perceptions for accuracy.

However, there are many ways to achieve the same results. Be sur to be clear on your goals, and then be flexible on the methods use to achieve them.

Principle

Flexibility

People can achieve their goals and outcomes in many different ways – thus the Centre for Strategic Management's "strategic consistency – operational flexibility" concept for the 21st Century.

Hold a "Debriefing" meeting with all key participants involved in an project or issue. Even if you have just one hour, use the standar Debriefing Agenda, illustrated in this tool, to maximize learning an improvements for the future.

EXAMPLES

Tool #8: Debrief All Projects/Conflicts

▶ **Workplace example:**

"Lesson Learned" is a common phrase in business referring t mistakes we've made that had a negative outcome. When dealin with a project that plays out over time, even small mistakes, mad early on, can have a huge impact down the road. One form thes mistakes often take are decisions made at the beginning of project that turn out to be very expensive. When do you cut you losses and decide to take a different approach (a different desig material or location), which seems like losing ground, but will hav a better long-term outcome?

At life and play example:

A move? A holiday party? An anniversary gathering? A family reunion? If you're reaction is "I'll never do THAT again!" do yourself a favor and debrief it, instead of dismissing it!

Chances are, you WILL have a chance to do it again. So you might as well make a few notes about what worked and what didn't! What questions do you wish you'd asked the caterer? What items do you wish you'd packed together for the move?

What logistics do you wish you'd considered for the reunion (Carpools? Handicapped access? Vegetarian meals? Laundry services?) If nothing else, you can pass these tips along to the NEXT host or family member who's moving! Let others learn from your debriefing, too.

USES

▶ Expand upon the three questions in Tool #7 by using mor extensive debriefing. The following are good opportunities:
1. Project Completion
2. Specific Big Incidents or Failures
3. Multi-day Workshops
4. Postmortems of Results from Big Issues or Problems
5. Conflict Situations
6. Cutbacks or Reorganizations

▶ **Debriefing Agenda:** Review the following five questions wit your team.

Debriefing Agenda	
1. Goals:	What were our multiple objectives? Any common objective?
2. What:	What happened in the project (pros and cons)?
3. So What:	So what did we learn (brainstorm)?
4. Now What:	Now what should we do differently in the future? a. To correct the problem if you need to b. To prevent it in the future
5. Celebrate:	How do we celebrate and recognize our project's success?

▶ Use the **Systems Thinking Assessment Questionnaire (A-B-Cs)** on the following page for additional debriefings, such a:

■ Revisiting your project plan after completion.

■ Preparing for an entire project, from the beginning, as a way t properly plan and test for completeness.

ystems Thinking Assessment Questionnaire (A-B-Cs)

A] 1. *Where do you want to be in your Ideal Future?* Your goals, purpose, mission, ends, outcomes, destination, etc. Did you make it?

B] 2. *How will you (did you) know when you get (got) there?* How do you know you are there now? (Use a quantifiable and measurable feedback system.)

C] 3. *Where are you now?* (Use today's assessment of status, SWOT: internal strengths and weaknesses plus external opportunities and threats, critical issues or problems.)

D] 4. *How do (did) you get there?* What actions did you take to close the gap from today to your Ideal Future in a holistic and strategic way? Is there still a gap?

5. *What were the Change Management structures and processes needed* to ensure that the actions and results above are achieved? Were they adequate?

E] 6. *Ongoing: What is/will/may/did change in your future environment* that can affect this project?

TOOL #8 SUMMARY

**Debrief All Projects/Conflicts:
Learn from your experiences!**

"Do you have ten year's experience?

-or-

One year's experience ten times?"

TOOL #8: Debrief All Projects/Projects

Worksheet #8

Debriefing

At Work or Play

1. Pick any project, conflict, issue or workshop you have resolved in your life recently:

_____

_____

2. Debrief in full below (involve key stakeholders?):

A Did you achieve your Ideal Future?

_____

_____

B How did you know when you got there?

_____

_____

C Where are you now (current status today)?

_____

_____

D How did you get to your results? Were you happy with them?

_____

_____

What were the Change Management structures and processes you used? Were they what was needed?

_____

_____

E Ongoing: What future environmental changes can affect this result negatively?

_____

_____

TOOL #9:

"What," "Why?" and "So What?"

For each problem ask: "What, Why & So What?" to get at the root causes and implications for the future.

TOOL #9: "What," "Why" & "So What?"

Probing Questions

Whenever you are involved in assessing an issue, a problem, or eve
a new opportunity, how do you learn to identify the total system imp
cations or relationships across the organization.

▶ How do all the parts relate to each other in a complex system

▶ How do they relate to the individual, department, or organization
   goals and vision?

▶ Do you ask the right questions to determine the correct path to take?

▶ Are you aware that delay time and delayed reactions caus
   inaccurate diagnoses and solutions?

▶ Did you know that direct cause and effect is a false environmen
   tally-free concept?

▶ Do you continually seek and understand the "roots" of an issue
   not just the symptoms?

Principle

Causes And Effects Are Not Closely Related

Delay-time and delayed reactions
cause inaccurate diagnoses and solutions.
Cause and effect are not as closely related in time and space
as most people think.

The following sets of questions give you a very simple and versatil
tool on how to structure your own thinking, those of others, or
group problem-solving effort when dealing with complex organiza
tional issues.

It will keep you away from the "quick-fix," analytic, knee-jerk "on
best-way," simplistic cause and effect response.

Are You A Strategic Thinker?

Be A Detective!

"What you look at is what you see."

"What you look for is what you find."

"What theory you use determines what you look for."

The following sets of questions give you a very simple and versatil
tool on how to structure your own thinking, those of others, or
group problem-solving effort when dealing with complex organiza
tional issues.

It will keep you away from the "quick-fix," analytic, knee-jerk "on
best-way," simplistic cause and effect response.

**Starting from where you are on a problem (or opportunity), as
three sets of questions:**

A. *Beginning Questions—What?*
1. *What* are your Goals? Vision? Purpose?
2. *What* helps you achieve these goals?
3. *What* hinders you from accomplishing more?
4. *What* helps you accomplish more?

B. *Follow-up Root Causes Questions—Why? & So What?*
1. *Why* does it happen?
2. *So what* is the result or outcome if it continues?

C. *Rewards and Consequences*
1. *So what* are the consequences of not improving this issue
2. So what rewards and recognition are appropriate?
3. So what are the negative consequences of non-performance

EXAMPLES _____

Tool #9: "What?," "Why?" and "So What?"

▶ **Workplace example:**
"Layoffs have been announced at my company. The workforce
up in arms! They can't DO that to us! We're going to FIGHT this
Sound familiar? A common reaction. What other kind of reactio
might there be?

Start by asking "What?" (Is the company trying to get rid
people? NO! The company is trying to reduce expenditures!)

"Why?" (Are sales down? Are costs up? Has a competitor ha
found a much more efficient way to do the same thing?)

"So What?" (So, we can fight losing our jobs...and maybe run the company out of business and ALL lose our jobs, or MAYBE we can help the company find some serious ways to cut costs and at least save SOME of our jobs!

After all, who knows more about what it takes to make our product than WE do? Or maybe we can all take a 10% cut in pay instead of losing 10% of the workforce, or maybe we can all reduce our hours 10%. Hey team, let's talk about this!

At life and play example:

"Pick your fights." Better advice was never given. Your neighbor has decided to put up a fence. You're furious.

Start by asking yourself "What?" (Is it going to be a high, ugly monstrosity or a low, tasteful eye catcher?)

Then ask "Why?" (Is there something you could do to help keep kids or dogs out of his yard?)

And finally "So What?" (Will your garden still get sun? Might it complement your new siding? Will it improve property values? Could it create a backdrop for the roses you've always wanted?)

THEN decide how you will approach your neighbor, asking how you might be involved in the planning of the fence (remember Tool #6... People support what they help create!). Now just think how valuable this tool might be if your son decides to go to school with green hair!

USES

The assessment form on Worksheet #9 is very powerful and can be used for most any issue. It "cuts to the chase" to uncover root causes and the serious consequences of not resolving them. Use it to increase the chances of successful problem-solving.

O—🔑

TOOL #9 SUMMARY

Be a detective to really get at the bigger picture that surrounds an issue. Look for the root causes and also look at all the broader environment, organizational factors and implications around the issue.

TOOL #9: "What," "Why?" and "So What?"

Worksheet #9

At Work or Play

1. List a complex issue you have in your organization or life:

_____

2. Answer the three questions in the order shown below:

3	1	2
Why is it occurring? ← Root Causes	**What** are the issues? →	**So what** are implications?

3. Now, create an Action Plan describing what to do:

	What to do?	By Whom?	By When?
1.			
2.			
3.			

Advanced and Complex Project Planning

TOOL #10:

Stakeholder Analysis (Conduct Open Systems Project Planning)

For each complex problem ask:

1. *"What are the demands of each stakeholder?"*

2. *"What are our responses today?"*

3. *"What should our responses be?"*

TOOL #10: Stakeholder Analysis

Advanced and Complex Project Planning

Today's project teams and organizations exist in a very comple[environment. In order to make sense of it all, use Systems Thinking

First, develop your ideal future vision of the project.

Next, make a list of specific stakeholders who may be impacted [the project (both internal and external to the organization). Focu especially on external stakeholders such as clients, customers, su[pliers, interest groups, community members, family members, churd groups and the like.

Then ask three simple, key stakeholder analysis questions:
1. "What are the demands made on us by EACH stakeholder?
2. "What are our responses today?"
3. "What should our responses be?"

This "Stakeholders Analysis" gives you more and better information 1 problem-solve, action plan, and succeed in your project.

Try to understand the system and its environments first. Organiza tions are open systems and viable only when they are adapting 1 their changing environment.

Principle

Understand Systems Holistically –
In Their Environment

Systems, and organizations as systems, can only be understood holistically. Try to understand the system and its environment first. Organizations are open systems and, as such, are viable only in mutual interaction with, and adaptation to, the changing environment.

Very often, one department (such as Finance or HR) can destroy team's efforts if it is unwilling to cooperate in funding a project (participate in simplifying policies. Within a cross-functional tear project, each team member has his or her own goals. Be sure 1 discover their goals and agendas and take them into account. Thi last step is vital to the success of the team's vision.

Our Complex World Today!

This "Open Systems Project Planning" or "Stakeholders Analysis"
crucial when dealing with large, complex projects such as downsizing
restructuring, becoming customer or market-oriented, changing enter
prise technology, installing intra/extranets, building factories, etc.

EXAMPLES

Tool #10: Conduct Open Systems Planning

▶ **Workplace example:**

This is an exercise in "How Big Can You Think?" Inadvertent
leaving a stakeholder out of planning a major change often cause
serious barriers to change implementation: 1) resistance yc
hadn't planned for and 2) unintended consequences you hadr
designed for. Either of these can be enough to completely dera
a change project. A little time and energy invested early on,
making sure your list of stakeholders is complete, is time well sper

▶ **At work and play example:**

Do you have a vision and a plan for the rest of your life? *"The re*
of your life" is a key stakeholder in every decision you make toda
which job or promotion to accept, how to finance your child'
college education, whether or not to adopt a pet, etc. If you dor
have a plan, how do you know you're going to end up where yc
want to be? If you don't have a vision of the future, how do yc
know if the choice you're about to make is moving you closer t
or further from, your ideal? Your vision for the future may be on
of the key stakeholders in your life decisions. Who are the ke
players in your Vision? Are they involved?

○━━ᵐ
TOOL #10 SUMMARY

For complex change projects, always identify the key
stakeholders before beginning a project.

Then, analyze their demands on the project and your current
responses to them. Are your responses adequate?

Worksheet #10

At Work or Play

Conduct Open Systems Project Planning:

1. Identify the main systems level your project is focusing on. List it here and in the center of diagram below:

_____

2. Next, have a clear Ideal Future Vision and list it here:

_____

_____

3. Identify all the key stakeholders for your project. List them on the diagram below on the spokes of the circle.

_____

4. Now fill out a detailed analysis of your stakeholders on the next page.

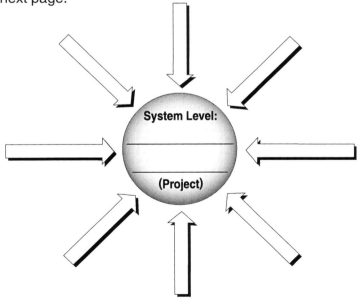

System Level:

_____

(Project)

Open Systems Planning — Stakeholders Analysis

Stakeholders (List)	Their wants and demands (on you)?	Your responses (today)?	Changes we need to make (for the future)?
1.			
2.			
3.			
4.			
5.			
6.			
7.			
8.			

Do You Know
What Is Important
To Each Member of Your
"Family"?

About the Centre

The Centre for Strategic Management®, founded in 1990, is a unusual mix of master level consultants, as Partners and Princ pals, across the globe, with 38 offices in 20 countries www.csmintl.com.

OUR CENTRE'S VISION

We are a leading-edge global alliance of diverse, master consultant and trainers. We are recognized and sought after for our unique Sys tems Thinking Approach™ to Creating Customer Value…our onl business.

ABOUT THE AUTHOR

Steve Haines is a CEO, entrepreneur, and strategist. He is als a facilitator and systems thinker as Founder and CEO of th Centre. He is a prolific author (14 books in print) an internationally recognized as the world leader in System Thinking and Strategic Management. He has an Ed.D. (A.B.D in Management and an M.S.A. in Organization Behavior with minor in financial management. He has over 30 years o executive experience leading planning, leadership, and chang efforts in the U.S., Canada, and globally. Steve is a U.S. Nav Academy engineering graduate, former Naval officer, and wa president and part owner of University Associates. He was als EVP at Imperial Corporation of America, and a member of eigh top management teams in his career.

Insightful – Passionate – Provocative

Contact Steve Haines at: Stephen@csmintl.com
- or -
through his website, www.StephenHaines.com

How To Order

Date _____ If Rush Order, need products by_____

Name _____ Title _____

Company _____

Shipping Address _____

City _____ State/Province _____

Country_____ Zip/Postal Code _____

Phone _____ Fax _____ Email _____

Qty.	Code	Description	Price	Amount
	HB-1	Daily Problem-Solving	Call	

Call for Quantity Discount Pricing	Sub total	
	Sales Tax (CA residents only)	
	Shipping/handling charges (min. $5.00—we will complete)	
	TOTAL (*payable in U.S.$*)	

TO ORDER

SYSTEMS THINKING PRESS®

Mail: 1420 Monitor Road, San Diego, CA 92110-1511 USA

Phone: (619) 275-6528

Fax: (619) 275-0324 (24 hours per day, 7 days per week)

Email: info@systemsthinkingpress.com

WWW **Website: www.systemsthinkingpress.com**